Hard to Please

Nick Warburton

Illustrated by John Rogan

OXFORD
UNIVERSITY PRESS

Nice buns, good buns

Mr Bodney the Baker was busy loading his van with buns and cakes.

'Rodney!' he called. 'Where are you?'

Rodney was in his room. He was half asleep and half awake. He was staring at the wall and thinking about his inventions. Something clever to make Bodney's buns the best around. Or something wonderful to keep the bread warm in the van.

'RODNEY!'

Rodney jumped up and clattered downstairs.

'Rodney, Rodney,' said Mr Bodney. 'Have you forgotten? Today's the day we take the buns to the Charles Brothers' Charming Tea Shop. If they like them, they'll sell them for us.'

'They'll like them, Dad,' said Rodney.
'I know they will.'

But Mr Bodney didn't look so sure.
The Charles Brothers were hard to
please. Everyone knew that. Still, he
bundled the last of the buns in the
back of the van and bundled Rodney in
the front. Then he started the van and
off they went.

Chuck Charles was waiting for them at the door of his Charming Tea Shop. He looked at his watch and tapped his foot. He was a short man with a long face. Chuck hated wasting time. And he never wasted his time by smiling.

Chick Charles was in the Tea Shop,
dusting some grubby old tables. He
looked up and saw Mr Bodney, but he
didn't smile. He never smiled, and he
never, ever laughed.

Mr Bodney put two plump buns on
two plates. Chuck took a nibble, Chick
chewed a crumb. They both looked sad
and sorry.

'Not bad,' said Chuck. 'Not bad.'

'But how much will they cost?' asked Chick.

Mr Bodney named his price.

'Too much, too much,' the Charles Brothers said together. 'Nice buns, good buns, but we can't afford them. We have to pay for the tea and we have to pay for the shop. We have to pay for the chairs and tables, and we have to pay to keep them clean.'

Poor Mr Bodney sighed and shook his head. The Charles Brothers would not sell his buns.

'I can help with that,' said Rodney.

'How?' asked Chick keenly.

Rodney didn't know, but he thought hard and he thought quickly. And an idea popped into his head.

'I have got a machine that will keep your tables clean,' he said.

Chuck looked at Chick and pulled a miserable face. Chick pulled a miserable face back.

'All right,' they said. 'Bring it along and we'll take a look.'

Buzz One
and the rice pudding

When Rodney got back to the bakery,
he went straight to his room and
started work on a clever and wonderful
machine. He shut himself away for
days, and puzzled and thought and
tinkered around. Sounds of banging
and clanking came from his room.
And at the end of a week he flung open
his door.

'It works! It works!' he cried. 'Come and look!'

Mr Bodney came to look. He saw a sort of dustbin on wheels with bits of wire sticking out of it. It had one long arm with a wet sponge on the end. When Rodney switched it on, the arm swished from side to side.

'I shall call it Buzz One,' said Rodney happily.

Next day they loaded Buzz One into the van and took it to the Charming Tea Shop. Chuck and Chick sat down on two battered old chairs. They folded their arms and made glum faces.

'Be amazed,' said Rodney Bodney, and he switched it on.

Chick and Chuck were amazed. The machine juddered and jolted and swept a plate of rice pudding off one of the grubby tables. Half went into Chuck's lap and half went into Chick's. It made a terrible mess.

'You fool!' Chick shouted. 'Just look at our trousers!'

'But it nearly worked,' Rodney said.

'Get out! Get out!' shouted Chuck.

Back at the bakery, Rodney thought hard for an hour or two. He thought about the rice pudding and he thought about Chuck and Chick. Then he thought about the two battered old chairs they sat on and all the grubby tables, and he had a new idea.

He shut himself away again and worked harder than ever. A week went by. Mr Bodney heard plenty of banging and hammering coming from his room.

Then the banging stopped, and there stood a large tin box with coloured lights on the top and wheels on the bottom. There were coils of wire coming out of the sides in a tangle. At the end of three long metal arms were three paint brushes – large, medium and small.

Mr Bodney listened outside the door. He heard Rodney singing as he put a coat of paint on his new machine. A dib here and a dab there. A dib on the tin box and a dab on his pyjamas. A dab on the metal arms and a dib on his cheek.

Then Rodney flung open the door and fell over his dad.

'Just look at this,' he said, jumping up.

Mr Bodney looked and blinked.

'Dad,' said Rodney, 'meet Buzz Two, the Paint Machine. Buzz Two, say hello.'

The lights on top of Buzz Two flashed on and off, as if it was saying hello.

'The Charles Brothers need nice bright tables and this machine will make painting easy,' Rodney explained. 'I tell it what to do and it does it. If I say p-a-i-n-t the table it will do just that.'

Rodney had to spell out the word 'paint'. If he said it properly, Buzz Two would go ahead and paint. The wonderful and clever thing about this machine was that it worked by the sound of Rodney's voice.

'Shall we try it out?' he said. 'Shall we get Buzz Two to paint my table?'

At once the metal arm with the large brush began to whirr and twizzle.

'Stop, Buzz Two,' said Rodney with a clap of his hands. 'We're not ready yet.'

And the machine stopped.

The last of the paint had been used to paint Buzz Two, so Rodney dashed into the kitchen and came back with a tin of syrup.

'This is a bit like paint,' he said. 'Buzz Two won't know the difference.'

He poured the syrup into the top of the tin box and stood back.

'Buzz Two, paint the table top,' said Rodney.

And the machine began to whirr and twizzle again. The lights came on and off and the brush-arm dipped itself into the syrup and began to paint. There was syrup all over Rodney's table top, where it was supposed to be, but there was syrup in lots of other places, too. Rodney and his dad had to crouch behind a chair until Buzz Two had finished.

'Now we need a machine to wipe up the syrup,' moaned Mr Bodney.

'But it works, Dad,' Rodney sang, skipping about in the puddles of syrup. 'It really works and it'll work for Chick and Chuck. Then they'll be pleased and they'll buy our buns!'

'If you say so,' said his dad, but he didn't sound so sure.

The next day Mr Bodney told Chick and Chuck all about the Paint Machine and how wonderful and clever it was. They hummed and grumbled and frowned at each other.

'Wonderful and clever, is it?' asked Chuck.

'And it doesn't throw rice puddings about?' said Chick.

Mr Bodney promised that it didn't.

'All right,' said the brothers. 'We'll come and look at it.'

Buzz Two
gets to work

At seven o'clock that evening they were knocking on the bakery door. Rodney let them in and smiled at them as sweetly as he could. They didn't smile back.

Rodney showed them up to his bedroom. Dad was waiting for them with a nervous grin. He had a brand new tin of red paint at the ready.

Rodney poured the red paint into the top of Buzz Two, switched on and crossed his fingers.

'Buzz Two,' said Rodney, 'paint the table.'

The big brush swished up and down and from side to side. In no time at all the table was shining red. Chuck's eyes grew wide as he watched the Paint Machine at work.

'Amazing!' he said. 'This could save us pounds and pounds at the Tea Shop.'

Then a shifty look came over his face.
'Does it only do tables?' he said. 'Can it do chairs?'

'Oh yes,' said Rodney, 'it can do chairs all right. Just watch.'

He grabbed a chair and stood it in front of the Paint Machine. Then he cleared his throat.

'Buzz Two, paint the chair.'

Buzz Two hummed and flashed its lights… but it didn't move.

'It doesn't work!' said Chick and Chuck together.

'It needs more instructions,' Rodney said. 'It's only done tables so far. Buzz Two,' he said. 'Paint the legs!'

And this time the Paint Machine began to move. It changed to the small brush and began dabbing paint on the nearest leg at high speed.

'Oh dear,' said Rodney. 'This isn't quite right.'

And it wasn't quite right. Buzz Two was painting the nearest leg, just as it had been told to do, but the nearest leg didn't belong to the chair. It belonged to Chuck Charles.

Chuck squealed like a pig and tried to hop out of the way. But Buzz Two wheeled after him and kept on painting. One of Chuck's legs was already red, and the machine was starting to move to the other one.

'Do something!' yelled Chuck Charles.

'Yes, yes, of course,' said Rodney. 'Buzz Two, paint the seat!'

Buzz Two stopped painting Chuck's legs and started painting his seat.

'No, no,' shouted Mr Bodney. 'The seat of the chair! Come on, Buzz Two. Stop messing about!'

But it was too late. Chuck Charles had two red legs and one red seat. And he did not look pleased.

'Oops,' said Rodney. He couldn't think of anything else to say.

Then he heard a strange sound. A wheezing, bubbling, cackling sound. He thought it was coming from Buzz Two but it wasn't. It was coming from Chick. Tears were running down his face and he was...

LAUGHING.

It was the first time anyone had ever seen Chick laugh.

'Oh dear,' he laughed. 'Oh dear, oh dear! I've never seen anything so funny in all my life. Oh Chuck, you must see the funny side.'

Chuck looked at his red legs and felt his wet red seat with his fingers.

'It's not funny,' he growled. 'Not funny at all.'

'It is, it is!' screamed Chick, rocking backwards and forwards and holding his sides.

'We'll see about that,' said Chuck grimly. 'Buzz Two, paint the ears!'

The machine buzzed and flashed.
It jerked back to life and started to roll
towards Chick.

'Ow!' yelled Chick. 'Ow, ow, ow!'

He tried to duck out of the way but it
was too quick for him. Slop! One red
ear. Slap! Two red ears.

'Hah!' shouted Chuck. 'Now paint
the nose!'

Buzz Two went to work on Chick's
nose.

'Ow! Ow, ow, ow!'

Then, very slowly, the sides of Chuck's mouth began to twitch. He gave a little snort.

And Chuck was laughing, too!

'Oh dear, oh dear,' chortled Chick. 'What a wonderful machine! We must have one, Chuck.'

'Yes, we must,' laughed Chuck. 'And we must have lots of Mr Bodney's buns, too.'

Buzz Two was a great success with customers at the Charming Tea Shop. When Mr Bodney and Rodney delivered their buns, they liked to stop and watch it working.

'It's a great machine, Rodney,' said Mr Bodney. 'Well done.'

It was so successful that the tables and chairs had to be painted several times over. Of course, sometimes it went a bit wrong and painted Chick or Chuck. But that made everyone cheer and clap and laugh out loud.

On most days you could hear laughter from the Charles Brothers' Charming Tea Shop. But no one laughed louder or longer than Chuck and Chick Charles themselves.

About the author

While I was teaching,
I enjoyed drama and reading
books aloud with children.
This encouraged me to write
and since then I have
written a number of scripts
for radio, stage and
television, around a baker's
dozen or so – that is, thirteen – children's
books. I do like sticky, syrupy flans and buns
too, although I can't ever remember
inventing anything.

I enjoy reading, almost anything to do with
cricket, and cycling around Cambridge,
where I live with my family.